WONDERLAND

Crónicas of Belonging in América

WONDERLAND

Crónicas of Belonging in América

Melanie Márquez Adams
Translated by Emily Hunsberger

Wonderland: Crónicas of Belonging in América

Cover Art: Octavio Quintanilla, Frontexto 307, "Los días oscuros" series, Acrylic on paper
Cover Design: Enzo Rodríquez Suárez
Interior Design: Kimberly James

ISBN 978-1-957840-36-9

Library of Congress Control Number
2 0 2 4 9 5 0 7 3 2

Published in the United States, 2025

$18

MOUTHFEEL PRESS

To Tennessee,
my mountain home,
mi querencia.
- M.M.A.

CONTENTS

"When I used to read
fairy tales, I fancied
that kind of thing never
happened, and now here I
am in the middle of one!
There ought to be a book
written about me, that
there ought! And when I
grow up, I'll write one..."

- Lewis Carroll, *Alice in Wonderland*

A Word from the Author

It's the fall of 2021, the start of my third semester at an MFA program for creative writing, my second year in the land of eternal ice and tornados. My second year away from my home in Tennessee. I've just walked out of a workshop (or was it one of the Spanish classes I have to teach to unenthusiastic freshmen?) when an email notification pops up on my phone. At first glance, it seems like yet another spam message. Inertia propels me to open it. It's supposedly from a literary agency in New York City. Yeah right, I think. Scam, much? But when I get to the end of the message, I start to consider the idea that it might be real. Once I get to my studio apartment in a corner house painted a shade of red that screams for the kind of attention I prefer to avoid, I Google the name of the agency and the person who wrote the email. I confirm that it is, in fact, a legitimate message. I read it again, this time with a bit more interest and a touch less cynicism.

The literary agent read a story of mine that appeared in the young adult fiction section of a well-known digital literary magazine. I have mixed feelings about this particular story; its publication me dejó un mal sabor de boca, the only time I've ever experienced such a sensation about my own work. It's a fictional story, una historia de dolor, based on the very real suffering of a little boy I met in a small town in Tennessee when I served as his mother's interpreter at a therapist's office. It's a story that I wrote, more than anything, to come up with a happy ending for a kid I would never see again. A purely cathartic exercise chock full of moralistic clichés.

The agent says that she and her boss loved my style and my voice and want to see more work like this from me. I reply saying that I have other work that might interest them, nonfiction pieces about my experience as an immigrant. The story in question was a unique text and I don't have anything else in that genre. But the agent wants nothing to do with my other work. The only thing she's interested in are predictable stories about immigrant pain and suffering, pandering to the demand for trauma porn starring el dolor inmigrante, apparently a highly addictive substance for certain readers. Nightmare border crossings through rivers and deserts to reach the American dream? The books become bestsellers, and, once something becomes "what people like to read," it starts being produced on a massive scale, reinforcing the idea that it must be the universal immigrant story. A vicious, self-fulfilling cycle. And a harmful one, too, in my opinion.

The exchange with the agent merely serves to stoke the flames of something that's been troubling me: the idea that my story as a latinoamericana that immigrated to a microscopic town in East Tennessee is one of privilege that doesn't deserve to be told. Who am I to contribute to the collection of immigrant narratives when I haven't suffered in the way others and their ancestors have? And to complicate things even further, my most important writing that's been published has been in Spanish. I'm bilingual, and even though I've read the classics of Latin American literature, a tally of my reading would probably show more books in English than Spanish, especially when it comes to creative nonfiction. Y sin embargo, he elegido escribir en español. ¿Por qué?

At first glance, the reason why I write in Spanish seems simple. It's my first language. It's the natural choice, no? But over time and as I learn more, I've come to realize that it goes much deeper than that. In reality, it's a conscious decision I make when I revise a text, whose first draft may have been in Spanish or English (or sometimes a little of both). As I further mold it into shape, the final version is almost always in Spanish, even though it's undeniable that, despite the over 40 million Spanish speakers that live in this country, the mainstream publishing world is utterly anchored in English. Even the books that big publishing houses commission to be translated into Spanish are mainly in the religious or self-help categories. Y claro, this reality leads me to question whether or not it's really worth it to tell a story that doesn't meet industry appetites, in a language at which they turn up their noses. Why even try?

And what's more, who am I to write in a language that isn't accessible to many Latinx writers because of pain, suffering, and shame related to their experience as immigrants? El dolor, siempre el dolor. The trials and tribulations I face as an immigrant don't carry the same weight of trauma. Can my nonfiction writing even be considered an immigrant narrative? Doubts upon doubts upon doubts.

It will take time to eventually quiet these thoughts and realize that my story, like all the others, is a piece with a unique place in the intricate rompecabezas that is immigration in the US. It's different, yes, but perhaps that's precisely why it deserves to be told. It complements and complicates the conversation (something all good literature is supposed to do). I'll come to discover that all the stories I've told and have yet to tell habitan y penan within me, alongside all the stories I've heard from others. Stories of joy and melancholy, shades of dark and light and gray. Situations and landscapes I observe and explore, that constantly challenge and surprise me. They keep me on my toes, nudge me over the precipice, and pick me up again. It's from this inner universe that I extract the threads to weave together the crónicas of my life in this country, mi nuevo hogar, my adopted Home. My Wonderland.

- Melanie Márquez Adams

January 2024

Translated by Emily Hunsberger

A Word from the Translator

The place we know as the United States is home to speakers of many different languages, and it always has been. Spanish, in particular, has been spoken here for over 500 years. Spaniards first arrived in Puerto Rico in 1493 and Florida in 1513, while their countrymen did not land in Ecuador, where Melanie Márquez Adams was born, until 1526. To put it another way: the Spanish language was first uttered in what is now known as the United States *before* its arrival in what is now known as Ecuador. In fact, the crónica is a genre of writing that dates back to accounts written by these European Spanish men about their exploratory and exploitative journeys in the Americas. In modern times, however, the crónica has evolved into a Latin American nonfiction genre that blends journalism, travel writing, and personal essay. Or in Melanie's personal interpretation: the White man chronicled the geography of *the other*; she chronicles the geography of *otherness*.

Today, while the majority of those of us that live in the US speak English, our community of Spanish speakers is still an order of magnitude larger than the rest of our minoritized linguistic communities. The United States is also home to a growing number of writers like Melanie, who speaks Spanish and English but does not write in both languages in equal measure. She prefers Spanish as her instrument of expression, but the English-language culture she inhabits finds its way into her writing. Similarly, Spanish finds its way into my English translations of Melanie's crónicas about her life as an immigrant, a woman, and a writer living in different parts of the United States, particularly the South, where she wrote and published work throughout the last two decades. Melanie and I live in the same country, in different cities but in similar worlds, where these two languages intermingle, se abrazan, give each other quizzical looks, and together forge something new they could never have created on their own.

While working on this book, I wrestled with an apparent contradiction in my decision to translate Melanie's work into English, since she and many of her fellow bilingual writers intentionally write in Spanish as an act of resistance. This is not something I wish to nullify or diminish, especially in a country where there are places it's not safe to speak Spanish in public, where Spanish can be used as a marker for linguistic and racial profiling, and where the mainstream publishing industry essentially turns a blind eye to domestic literature written in Spanish. What I have come to see, however, is that by bringing Melanie's work into English, I am able to relieve her from having to self-translate, as so many immigrants must do in their daily lives. And the fact that you, reader, are curious about the contents of this book also proves that the publication of a translation can lend legitimacy and a sense of importance to the work, while still calling your attention to the fact that it was written in Spanish *first*. It is my hope that the author's original act of resistance is echoed through my act of translation.

I also want to make special mention of the "choose your own

crónica" section of this book containing two alternative translations of an experimental text that Melanie wrote for *Enviado especial*, an anthology in which twenty Latina and Latino writers reflect on Cuba, edited by Hernán Vera Álvarez and published in 2022 by Suburbano Ediciones here in the United States. Melanie's essay was written in dialogue with fragments from a long poem by 20th-century Cuban poet Virgilio Piñera, "La isla en peso." In one version, I translated the slivers of Piñera's poem; in the other, I left his words untouched. In both versions, Spanish and English coexist, just like they do in Miami, a place that figures prominently in this particular crónica.

Miami is a point of connection and intersection for Melanie and me. It's where she first lived when she came to the US in the 90s as a college student, meanwhile I was a high school student living just an hour north of there. You see, as the translator of these crónicas, I am not importing the author's work de un lugar remoto y extraño, nor is the author's writing about an exotic land I can only imagine in my mind's eye. On the contrary, the author and I have shared and continue to share many spaces both physical and metaphysical; so much so that we thought it would be fitting to allow my presence to infiltrate the space of these texts from time to time. [*You'll find my words between brackets, like this, sometimes addressed to Melanie, the text itself, or you, the reader.*]

Consider the brackets little windows into our harebrained tea party in Wonderland.

- Emily Hunsberger
January 2024

Wonderland

Modern-day castles loom above the treetops and the flowery lab-
yrinths seem to go on forever. The contrast between the peaceful
mountain town I left earlier today and the opulence that now sur-
rounds me leaves me disoriented and a little dizzy. I take a deep
breath, close my eyes, and try to be present in the moment. After
all, I was inspired to come here by an adventurous little girl who
followed a white rabbit into a strange and different world.

I dive headfirst into Central Park. I walk past fountains, lakes, and
gardens until I finally arrive at my destination on East 74th Street: a
still-life version of what's arguably literature's most famous tea party.
I find myself face to face with Alice sitting atop a giant mushroom
and much more charming than the Google images made her seem.
Not to be missed are her whimsical companions, the White Rabbit
and the Mad Hatter. With its imponencia y magia, it's as if the statue
were inviting you to meld into the bronze and follow the characters
into a parallel dimension turned upside down. Children and adults
alike eagerly climb along the statue's curves, mimicking the squirrels
that leap among the branches of the surrounding oaks and pines.

I clean off a bench with a napkin to sit and watch, captivated by
how Alice plays hostess to the guest-tourists. It's a nice day out and
everyone is smiling. Yo también. I'm waiting for an old classmate
that I haven't seen since our college days in South Florida. After we
graduated, I returned to Guayaquil and Carolina went back to her

native Brooklyn to reluctantly begin our adult lives. I made my best attempt for eight years. Now I'm back en el mundo universitario anglo, living in the South and pursuing a master's degree in literature.

Thanks to the North American phenomenon known as Spring Break, I was able to escape to this city containing every possible color and language, more specifically to this delightful tea party in Wonderland. My long-awaited guest arrives, algo nerviosa as she declares that she only has a thirty-minute break. I thank her for indulging my request to have a picnic in the park like New Yorkers in a sitcom. For the first ten minutes we catch up on our lives. I'm thrilled that Carolina is getting a master's in creative writing at NYU and disappointed she shows little interest in sharing more about it. When all that's left of my pastrami sandwich are a few crumbs, I break the awkward silence with the first thing that comes to mind: I ask her if she's ever read *Alice in Wonderland*. [Alicia en el país de las maravillas *is how you knew it as a child in Ecuador.*]

"No, I only saw the Disney movie," she replies as she places the lid back onto the plastic container of a neglected kale salad that seems to peer at me wiltingly. "It didn't really make sense."

"I never saw the movie, I only read the book. And you're right, the story doesn't make any sense, but I think that's the whole point . . ."

"As a kid I only read the books assigned to us in school, and—" We're interrupted by the shouts of kids playing and running around Alice. "Oh, that reminds me, I signed up for a workshop on literature for children and young adults. I've got writer's block, and I want to see if exploring a different genre will help me find my way out of this rut with my novel."

I try to dig a little deeper, asking what her novel is about, but Carolina only wants to talk about the workshop.

"What was your favorite book as a kid?" she asks. Something in the way she's looking at me tells me I should choose my answer wisely.

"Hmm, that's a hard one, the list is pretty long . . ." I search for the perfect answer in Alice's eyes. "Well, one of the books I remember fondly is *Little Women* . . ."

"The name rings a bell, but I'm not familiar with it. Are there any people of color in it?"

"Of color?" Perhaps I heard her wrong, what with all the noise coming from the pigeons and tourists.

Carolina senses my confusion and repeats the question, more *s l o w l y* this time, assuming that my non-native English is behind the puzzled look on my face.

"I understand what you're saying, but not the question," I continue. "What do you mean by 'of color?' The characters in *Little Women* are human beings, not colorful creatures."

I'm imagining electric-blue Smurfs and banana-yellow minions scurrying about the park, terrorizing the squirrels and the well-behaved perros neoyorquinos.

"No, you're not getting what I mean." My old classmate's water bottle lets out an unpleasant creak as she squeezes it with her hands. "I want to know if any of the characters are Black, Latino, or some other non-White race."

"Este . . . I don't really know if the novel mentions a specific race, but . . ."

"Where's the author from?"

"Louisa May Alcott . . . if I'm not mistaken, she's from Boston."

"Oof. I bet all the characters in the story are White just like her. I definitely can't use it for my workshop."

"Why not?" I protest, somewhat offended, not unlike the youngest sister in Alcott's book. "It's by a feminist author, who was a pioneer in her time. And one of the protagonists is a role model for girls who dream about becoming writers when they grow up."

"I'm not interested in stories about little White girls," she replies, looking askance at Alice. "Junot Díaz says that we shouldn't support literary white supremacy. You know who I'm talking about, right?"

I shake my head. I urgently need the rabbit to lend me his watch to see if Carolina's thirty minutes are up.

"He's a Dominican author who immigrated here when he was a kid. He's published novels, short stories, won the Pulitzer." My old college classmate's pupils could burn a hole in my face. "How is it that you've never read the work of one of the most important Latino writers in this country?"

"Pues, I'm not sure," I reply, practically apologizing. "His writing has never been assigned in any of the classes for my master's program. We mostly read works by long-dead Latin American and Spanish authors."

Carolina checks the time on her phone, not even bothering to conceal her irritation. Since time has practically slowed to a halt, I try to salvage the rest of the conversation. I ask her to tell me more about this author, since what he says seems to be important to her. Her face softens, and I feel myself relaxing a little.

"In this country, from the time we're little kids, they force literature written by White authors down our throats," she says in a professorial tone. "As people of color, we don't see ourselves in their stories and we can't relate to their characters. Listen for yourself."

A video appears on her iPhone screen. Carolina gives me her earbuds. I find it challenging to understand the author's perspective. I can barely follow what he's saying, distracted by the many *fucks* proceeding from his mouth, but the impatient face that's watching for my reaction forces me to concentrate. Between *fucks*, Díaz explains that every book he reads, and every movie he sees is essentially a version of *Lord of the Rings* where Middle Earth is inhabited by White people, and the themes they explore have nothing to do with "nosotros." I wonder if "nosotros" refers to Dominicans, Latinos, Hispanics, or all people of color in the United States . . . or all people of color around the world. A tumult of labels splays out before me, forming a landscape in which I'm not sure I belong.

I give Carolina her phone back. I can see sparks of triumph burning in her eyes, but the cold current of my skepticism promptly stamps them out.

"No entiendo," I say, ignoring the voice inside me telling me to drop the issue altogether. "Why does Junot Díaz read Frodo and the rest of the characters as Caucasian? They're not even human! Couldn't we interpret Tolkien's universe as a diverse world where fairies, elves, and hobbits coexist as creatures of different races?"

"The problem is that you didn't grow up here," she says with great exasperation. "That's why you don't understand what we're talking about. And I doubt you ever truly will. But you should know that if you want to become a writer in this country, you're going to have to identify as a writer of color. If not, you're never going to get anywhere."

Now is when I decide to keep quiet. This reencuentro has not turned out to be the much-anticipated reunion of two writerly souls in the city of all cities. We exchange a few lukewarm last words, referring to a possible brunch that both of us know will never materialize. We say goodbye with a halfhearted hug and I watch her fade into the swaths of people rushing in every direction.

I sit there un buen rato. My feet and my head aren't quite ready to keep up with the frenetic pace of the city. Question marks swirl around the sculpture of Alice until they arrange themselves into a riddle: Are you or are you not a writer of color? I see little girls of different races joining the tea party, laughing and posing in front of their parents' phones: an Alice in every color. Which of them would Junot Díaz have chosen to be the protagonist of the story?

I leave the creatures of the park behind, seduced by the allure of Fifth Avenue. Next stop: Tiffany's with its unabashed display of excess. The glittering precious stones in the shop windows manage to bring me back to earth and comfort me. Now I know why Truman Capote imagined this corner of the city as a sacred place for Holly Golightly. I gaze at an onyx stone surrounded by a string of pearls, and from its dark depths emerge even more questions: What if Holly Golightly's real name hadn't been Lulamae Barnes, sino Lupita Beltrán? And instead of fleeing a bleak little town in Texas, she had been hiding her infancia humilde in East L.A.?

As I leave that bewitching street corner behind, trying to shake

24

off the swirl of questions, I suddenly notice a short, stocky woman yelling and running in my direction. The roar of traffic and people scrambles her words, and for a moment it sounds like she's screaming, "Off with her head!" I accept my sentence. My head is about to explode, anyway. But the Queen of Hearts runs right past me and into a McDonald's.

Even though my feet are threatening mutiny, a leisurely pace is not an option. The New York rabbits push and pull me with their *I'm late! I'm late!* hustle. The smiling Cheshire cat-tourists appear and disappear, stopping in all the most inconvenient spots to take pictures of their *unvacation*, much to the torment of the rabbits. This scene repeats itself for several blocks until I reach Times Square, where time stops and stretches and clocks become useless. Where the world begins and ends. The psychedelic waves pulsing across the billboards threaten to suck me into their ebb and flow. [*The place, name and all, really does seem like a Lewis Carroll invention.*] I look to the heavens to beg for mercy, and the sky offers me a sunset bursting with pinks and oranges. That's enough for one day for this *uncity* girl.

I walk to the 42nd Street subway station. A filthy stairwell leads me down into the underbelly of this singular island-wonderland. In the subway car, where everyone is elbow to elbow but somehow pretending their fellow passengers don't exist, a few of the colorful creatures are reading. I wonder if their books and screens are really mirrors inhabited by their doppelgängers. I imagine the mirrors shattering into thousands of words telling stories in Spanish, English, French, and Mandarin—an army of runaway stories that have come to rescue me from the ambush of questions and reveal that the key to solving to the riddle lies within me, in the stories that are mine to write. I take out my notebook and begin, the train gently swaying as it makes its way through the cavernous tunnels, trusting that I will find the answer on the other side.

The Color of Lakes

"No, no. What's your *real* name?" she asks, completely unfazed, as if someone introducing themselves with a fake name were a routine occurrence.

"Este . . . I'm not sure what you mean." I start to wonder if the rules of the game have changed since I last navigated life as a college student in America.

"Well, a lot of international students choose to go by an American name, because, you know, their real names are hard to pronounce." She smiles, and her perfectly white teeth practically blend in with the vampiric hue of her pale skin.

I smile back. It's not the first time I've been told I don't look like a Melanie, and I'm sure it won't be the last.

"Of course, now I get it," I say, shaking my head perhaps a touch too emphatically.

While pointing to the glittery sign that's precariously affixed to my dorm room door, I explain that Melanie is in fact my real name and that when I was little, people back home in Ecuador were the ones who had a hard time pronouncing my name.

"Wow! Really?" She covers her mouth with her right hand as she laughs, her shoulders slowly moving up and down. Her pointy chin is the finishing touch: the spitting image of a cartoon villain.

It's nighttime, and I'm aimlessly pacing the kitchen, exhausted and famished after a three-hour class. Cindy comes out of her room, at the ready with indispensable college student provisions—cookies and candy—that she places in a plastic bowl doubling as a center-piece on the table.

She has all sorts of questions about where I come from. She wants to know about the weather, the food, the music. Most of all she's curious about the people that live in aquel rincón distante del mundo. "I bet life is more exciting there." Her eyes widen and shine as I tell her about Ecuador, like a little girl who just discovered a new animated series on TV.

Cindy has never left the country—she's never traveled more than a few states away from Tennessee. Her fascination with the for-eign-born began when she was in high school, where she connected with exchange students from Asia and Africa that had landed in her rural town. She's been hooked ever since.

Whenever she talks about the exchange students, her blue eyes start to glisten. The first time it happens, I gingerly ask if one of them passed away.

"No, it's not that," she says, swiping her knuckles underneath her eyes. "It's just that . . . they were all so *cute!*"

She reminds me of a little girl in a movie I saw once who cried inconsolably about a litter of puppies that she didn't want to give away. It was a shame; they were taken away from her just as she started to get attached.

I spend most of my time by Cindy's side. We go shopping at the only mall in town or at Walmart. Sometimes we go for a car ride and explore the mountains looking for a nice place to hike.

One cool, spring afternoon, we're walking beneath the pines, whose branches intertwine around us. Captivated by the squirrels and their acrobatics, I tell Cindy to imagine that something magical is happening: the lively squirrels are transforming into beautiful, languid iguanas that prefer to bathe in the sunlight rather than run around like maniacs.

"Can you see it, Cindy?" I ask expectantly. "Now you're in my hometown, Guayaquil!"

Her eyes grow as wide as two enormous blue balloons. I've never been able to delight someone so easily with my words.

One Wednesday night, she invites me to go to church with her. Wary, I tell her tactfully that my tolerance for sermons is limited to Sundays. Bueno, algunos domingos. I don't confess my irrational fear that, among the jelly doughnuts and danishes that abound in the fellowship halls of Baptist churches, there are tiny, hidden Catholic detectors cloaked in powdered sugar. What if the moment I enter the church, an alarm starts to go off and a pastor comes running from the pulpit to kick me out and tell me that my graven image-worshiping soul will never get to heaven?

"But Wednesday is college night!" she insists. "There's no sermon. It'll be fun, I promise." It's hard to imagine something church-related being fun, but it's impossible to say no to those pleading, puppy dog eyes.

We enter an auditorium bursting at the seams with teenagers and twentysomethings. A couple of men, barely older than the people in the audience, are wrestling with a bunch of cables and equipment on the giant stage. Before I can ask Cindy if we're at a church or a concert, darkness descends and the stage comes to life in neon colors that flash to the beat of the bass and electric guitar.

With her eyes closed and her arms lifted to the heavens, Cindy's body sways to the rhythm. The melody is catchy and the lyrics are easy to follow. I surrender to the voices of exaltation, and my own hips start to sway, poseídas por un espíritu embriagante.

We fill our trays in the student dining hall, where I've discovered my affinity for make-your-own waffles. We pass the time trying to spot international students we find attractive. One guy in particular—you guessed it, with dark skin, eyes, and hair—catches Cindy's eye.

Just before the sweet relief of spring break, I surprise her with some good news. I finally crossed paths with the guy from the dining hall. His name is Javier, and it turns out, he's from Mexico.

"I just knew he was Latino!" she shouts. "You have to introduce me! Pleeease!"

Clapping her hands together in excitement, she tells me she's always wanted to go out with a Latino guy.

"But why a Latino guy, Cindy?" I ask, even though I know the answer. Siempre es la misma respuesta. [*Wait for it . . .*]

"They're so *sexy*, so *romantic!*" [*. . . there it is.*] She bites her thin lower lip as she searches for something to add. "I don't know . . . White guys, they can be so *boring*. I want something different. Something exciting."

The turquoise waters of her eyes gleam with possibility.

Eight years later, I stumble upon Cindy's Facebook page only to find she's engaged to a guy that could pass for her brother. I guess the Latino boyfriend fantasy didn't make it to happily ever after. Neither did our friendship, which succumbed to the tensions of sharing an apartment. Or maybe it was the age difference. Or perhaps some friendships are only meant to last the sixteen weeks of an academic semester.

Whenever I think about those carefree spring days that I spent with Cindy, discovering my new surroundings, nestled among forests and mountains, I imagine her chatting with her current friends about the international student that was once her roommate. Her eyes, the color of the lakes that dot the landscape I now call home, glisten with memories of iguanas, squirrels, and Latino boyfriends.

Campus Selfie

I've landed in the middle of nowhere is my first thought, as I'm carted in a van from a miniature version of an airport to the college campus where I'll spend the next two years. My second thought is *I feel like a background character in a movie.* The kind of movie that takes place in one of those country towns with a single gas station and a general store at its center. One of those towns where everyone has known everyone else their whole lives.

As the weeks go by, I venture out into the landscape that unfurls like the green and blue squares of a quilt, the fabric stamped with mountains, lakes, forests, national parks, churches, farms, and fields. The pattern silently but relentlessly repeats itself, over and over. I need to check the GPS from time to time to avoid getting lost between the seams.

During the first week of my psychology class, the silver-haired professor, a dead ringer for Stephen King, asks me to visit his office. I've barely sat down when I come to find out I'm his first student from South America.

In this cubicle-office tucked away in a forgotten corner of the campus, I begin my tenure as a subject of anthropological study.

The professor takes pains to engage with the international students in his class. Whether we're learning about grieving rituals or family dynamics, it never fails that a *What are things like in your country?* will soon follow.

Most of the time, the student from China is the first to be subjected to interrogation. Then it's my turn, before we finish things off with a few anecdotes about dysfunctional families in India.

I'm embarrassed by the deflated look on the face of Stephen King's doppelgänger when I tell him that "down there," in the South America of his imagination, interpersonal interactions are not that different from those "up here." The anticipation fades from his small, light eyes, peering at me from behind rectangular frames.

Not wanting to further disappoint him, I surrender and begin to invent the type of fanciful, Macondo-esque stories I know he wants to hear.

The next semester, I enroll in a class about cultural memory. Between stories of Holocaust survivors and slave narratives, we read Rigoberta Menchú's autobiography.

I have a hard time understanding why I haven't read this book before. ¿Por qué, cuando por fin lo hago, tiene que ser en un salón de clases norteamericano?

The professor assigns chapters to each student to analyze and present to the rest of the class. My section contains moving accounts of the K'iché people's traditions. I learn that when a new member of the community is born, they are gifted with a small bag filled with garlic, lime, salt, and tobacco, as a form of protection.

I also learn that when children turn ten years old, the adults in the community share the history of their people with them to ensure that their cultural legacy is passed down to the next generation.

After the academic part of my presentation, where I dissect the text according to the theories we've studied, I share a personal reflection. Reading about K'iché culture has made me face the sad reality that I don't know anything about the indigenous traditions of my own country. If I'm familiar with a few Quechua words, it's merely because they've been incorporated into Ecuadorian colloquial speech. And apart from some interactions at artisan markets, I can't recall having an actual conversation with a person of indigenous origin.

I don't know if it's more sad than it is shameful. Solo sé que duele.

At the end of my first year living in East Tennessee, I collapse onto a bench, exhausted. Wrapped in an alpaca shawl, I observe the leafless beings that inhabit the grounds of the campus.

Despite the fact that their clothing has come apart and is disintegrating at their feet, the trees stand tall, waiting, unchanging, certain that in time they will become whole again.

Their determination reminds me that I also had to shed my protective covering—aquí en este extraño trozo de mundo—in order to find myself again.

I may be missing some leaves, but I'm on the right track.

Spring is right around the corner.

Appalachian Ballad

I change the station and the speakers tremble with the gruff voice of Johnny Cash. Driving through the rolling, blue mountains, country and gospel music are my only travel companions. As I turn the dial searching for something to match the mood, the frenzied voice of a preacher tries to overtake the music and tell me all the reasons why my soul needs saving. But Johnny wins the battle, and I end up singing along to "Walk the Line."

My mind pulses with the chorus, and I think of the line I constantly have to walk myself. But, unlike the one Johnny sings about, mine isn't straight. It twists and turns, like switchbacks on a mountain trail.

I turn up the volume and wonder how much longer it will take to get to my destination. It's hard to know exactly where I am. Maybe Kentucky or perhaps Virginia. Most likely, I'm still in Tennessee, but the borders and landscape blend together and confuse me. [*As you wrote before, "the pattern silently but relentlessly repeats itself, over and over."*] Just a few miles away, in the Cumberland Gap, you can stand at the point where the three states meet and still feel like you're nowhere in particular.

In the middle of this thought, an image appears in my mind's eye. It's a place that seems to be slipping further and further away from me these days: a spot marked by a white stripe where you can stand with each foot in a different hemisphere.

The two images crash together and become entangled. The dividing lines merge and separate over and over again in a complicated dance. I speed up my footwork, trying to keep up. I dance with the lines and around them. En los márgenes and somewhere in between.

It's hard not to step on the lines. Nearly impossible not to transgress them.

I lose myself in the song, and the notes reverberate with memories. An office job with a forty-minute commute; a string of buildings, traffic, and billboards. It starts to take a toll on me, so I begin a quest for a new soundtrack. My spirit of adventure awakens from its slumber, and I choose a remote southern city in a northern country. I convince myself that even though there are no big cities nearby, it's a college town, so I should be able to fit in without too much trouble. ¿Cierto?

A biting cold welcomes me when I first touch down one January afternoon. It's practically an affront compared to the stifling heat surrounding the beginning of my journey in the wee hours of the madrugada guayaquileña.

I had already begun to fret a few minutes after takeoff: how could I have forgotten to arrange a meeting point? What if the university representative is waiting for me at a different terminal in the airport? What if I miss the only form of transportation I have in a place where I don't know a soul?

All these questions fade away as a more pressing one rises to the surface, at the sight of the tiniest airport I've ever seen, barely visible amid a heavy blanket of snow.

¿Dónde he venido a parar?

Cloaked in haze, the buildings dissolve into mountains, the traffic into solitude, and the billboards into signs emblazoned with Bible verses. The verses are alternately comforting and... chilling. I turn the dial again: bluegrass. The instruments come into tune little by little until they begin to play me a personal mountain symphony.

The music of Appalachia leads me onto the floor in the dance-hall of memory.

The mandolin sings, and I'm transported to my first Easter dinner with a local family. After a heavy feast, the matriarch stands up from the table and announces that she's going to take an after-dinner walk. Without batting an eyelash, she adds that she's also going to look for snakes.

With a twang of the banjo, I suddenly find myself at my first town fair, overwhelmed by the dizzying smell of fry oil and the stares of a little snow-white blonde girl. The precocious curiosity in her eyes reminds me that she and I are not as different as we might think.

The violin squeals, and my eardrums strain the same way they do when I hear a southern accent in English. The instrument's strings mark the steps of a pointy-nosed old man I see dancing in Pigeon Forge—a handful of white tufts remaining on his head, vigorously determined to prove he's still got it. Quick and light on his feet, he gallops across the floor with a mix of Irish, or maybe Scottish, steps. An enormous silver belt buckle engulfs his fragile yet resilient body.

The husky melody of the acoustic guitar sends me to the middle of a college classroom. Once again, the professor [*Stephen King's dop-*

pelgänger] is asking me about the colorful postcard picture of a place from which he imagines I hail. The wild lyrics of the song playing in the background seem to remind the professor that he doesn't need to travel far from home for a taste of exotic folklore.

The bass groans and echoes across mountains and more mountains, endless railroad tracks, innumerable churches, never-ending American flags. The interminable chorus hypnotizes me and makes me long for the city where I was born, makes me miss the hectic waves of people, the skyline, the chorus of squawking car horns.

At times I feel like a city slicker stunned by the unmovable, leaden silence of rural life. But as the adrenaline from the savage pace of urban life slowly dissipates, something unexpected happens. Suddenly, it's the constant onslaught of people, noise, cars, and buildings piled one on top of another that overwhelms, exhausts, and suffocates me. El alarido incesante del tráfico swells and crescendos until I've lost myself completely and can no longer hear the sound of my own voice.

Through the tumultuous roar of Guayaquil, the mountains' melancholy song finds its way to me. Like sirens they draw me toward them, enticing me to join their chanting. The dividing lines push and pull me until I fall down, and I'm not sure which side of the border I'm on. I have no alternative but to get up and continue the complicated dance. I trust that the mountains will help me survive my slips and stumbles.

As my song comes to an end, the voices of Appalachia begin to hum. Their nostalgic ballads recount tales of coal mines, fracking, patchwork quilts, and the sting of moonshine in your throat. Of scraping by and simple joys. I listen and heed their call as they beckon me to my adopted country home.

There's a train a-coming, and its whistle resounds in tune with the melody.

Boardwalk Rhythm

Coney Island. Amor a primera vista, like an old flame from a past life. You're utterly captivated by this cosmos of shops, bars, and cafés strung between an amusement park and the sea.

The boardwalk.

A place to sit with an ice cream cone or a beer in hand. To bask in the sea breeze. To watch hundreds of tourists coming and going, boisterous as the hungry seagulls that hover around you.

Where you can walk into a bar and the bartender knows all the regulars by name. As if you walked through a portal to a long-lost memory belonging to algún abuelo.

Perhaps it's one of their childhood memories, because Coney Island has the soul of an old-time circus, a fantasy world permeated by the aroma of salt.

In place of popcorn in a red and white striped box, there's bottles of beer.

In place of the pipe organ, there's the cadence of the waves crashing against the pier.

The main event: the colorful ebb and flow of people as the wood planks reverberate with their accented chatter and laughter.

Old men with their fishing poles and nothing to prove. They're not out here to lord themselves over the sea creatures. They're looking for the same thing as the rest of us: to be part of the show, side characters in this world of whimsy.

On the other side of the country, the Santa Monica Pier. In the middle of the boardwalk, a troubadour Jesus strums the guitar to the delight of his half-moon of apostles. No one takes offense, it's all part of the buena onda.

At the end of the pier, signs tell the story of Olaf Olsen, a brawny sailor that spent his last days in this place, far from where he was born, the inspiration behind the endearing cartoon character Popeye the Sailor Man.

When you look at photographs of Olsen—the unmistakable mischievous smile and prominent jaw—there's no doubt in your mind the story is true. You rather enjoy standing in that spot, looking out onto the same corner of the Pacific that the brave seaman sailed long ago in search of adventure.

This is, after all, what made you fall in love with boardwalks. The vintage scent of possibilities from a time when a technology-filled future seemed impossibly far away. Cool air under the blue shade of the big top, where the only commandment is to sit back, relax, and catch a good vibe. To take in the dizzying array of shops and concession stands, like flashy clowns offering a never-ending supply of trinkets, rounds of shots for the whole crew, and most of all, memories. Moments tucked away in a magician's hat.

There they'll stay until one of those days when your technology-filled world is about to boil over with stress, and out of the corner of your eye you'll spot a vibrantly colored magnet on your refrigerator door.

In that moment, you'll remember your day by the sea, gliding along the old wooden planks, sin prisas, your feet stepping in time to the heartbeat of the waves. A stroll through a magical land of old, when the world was less complicated and moved to a boardwalk rhythm.

The Ghost of the South

They say that the halls of the palatial Opryland Hotel in Nashville, Tennessee are haunted by the ghost of a woman known as the Lady in Black. Those who have seen her maintain that this bone-chilling apparition dons a gauzy black dress: a perfect specimen of Southern Gothic style. The hotel staff assures their guests that the ghost is not to be feared, as she is content to simply observe the droves of tourists flocking to the hotel's opulent fountains and gardens.

Farther below on the same continent (or on a different one, depending on the country where you learned geography) stories are whispered about a similar specter, with the exception that this ghost doesn't settle for merely observing the living. She has a much more traditional approach to her occupation, and in her prime she took great pleasure in terrorizing the streets of Guayaquil. She's known as the Dama Tapada, a lady ghost who first began haunting Ecuador's largest city in the 1700s.

Nearly every version of the legend of the Dama Tapada describes her as a slender woman (when it comes to female spirits, their figures are almost always described as slender) with a dark veil covering her face. They say the Dama would begin her ghoulish labors at the stroke of midnight, setting out to seduce and entrap unsuspecting gentlemen leaving the city's taverns. At that hour, the gaslight lamps would cast a sinister glow onto the cobblestone streets: the perfect setting for a manhunt.

The poor drunken fellows lacked any self-control when faced with the seductive guile of a beautiful woman, and they would follow her down dark passageways and back alleys, as if in a trance. Once she had cornered her prey, the Dama Tapada would slowly lift the veil to reveal her face: a splendidly putrescent skull.

As in any good ghost story, the men either dropped dead from a heart attack after the terrifying encounter, or they would be forever marked by an indelible trauma (but not without the consolation prize of a hair-raising anecdote to frighten and impress their future grandchildren). Just imagine for a moment the panic that ensued as word spread about the hauntings: "¡Cuidadito, señores! This too could be your fate if you don't go straight home after work!"

Yet it seems the Dama Tapada grew tired of the streets of Guayaquil, and she was no longer seen in the port city. Sightings were reported sporadically in other parts of Ecuador and neighboring countries, but after a time, poof! Clearly a spirit that found such pleasure in haunting the land of the living wouldn't just decide to vanish at the drop of a hat—it makes no sense. On the contrary, the explanation may be far more simple:

Like so many of us, perhaps the restless Dama decided to go North.

After Felipe V decided to make El Callao the main port of the Spanish colonies in America, Guayaquil started to lose the glow that had once been so enticing to the Dama Tapada. The 1742 outbreak of yellow fever that wiped out half of the population must have been the final straw. What fun was there in spooking deserted streets? ¡Adios, Perla del Pacífico! It's easy to imagine the Dama exploring, over the decades, the streets of Florida, Alabama, and Georgia (all of which, as we know, are chock full of ghosts) until finally ending up in the capital of Tennessee. Buoyed by its status as a port city—and an important railroad hub, as well—Nashville started to grow significantly from 1779 on, something that did not go unnoticed by our spectral traveler.

Nor did one of the city's most attractive features: the Cumberland River running right through the middle of downtown. Let's not forget that the Dama carried the Río Guayas in her unbeating heart.

The star of the vibrant Southern capital continued to rise over the centuries, and the Dama Tapada gradually fell under its spell (remember, ghosts don't experience time the same way we do).

And there she stayed, strolling down the city streets filled with people and the sound of music at every turn; just the right amount of clamor and chaos, nothing like the great metropolises of Latin America and the United States, where even spectral beings find themselves crammed together, shoulder to shoulder.

In Nashville, there's room for everyone. *Welcome, y'all!* It doesn't matter if you're living or dead, you'll still be greeted with a shot of whiskey and a disarming melody.

Our Dama couldn't help but fall in love with country music: simple, infectious songs that tug at your heartstrings, evoking visions of hay bales, pick-up trucks, and broken hearts.

Despite her affection for Nashville, not even a phantom is above the rules and regulations of this country, and the authorities wouldn't recognize the Dama Tapada's Ecuadorian license to spook inebriated partiers. Over time, they also prohibited her from using her veil (careful, here they are suspicious of people based on head coverings alone), which led her to realize it didn't make sense to translate her name into English as the Veiled Lady. Fortunately, people have been changing their names for centuries upon arriving in this country, and, for a ghost, the sky's the limit when it comes to choosing a moniker. You're living the American dream, after all.

Welcome to the U S of A, querida *Lady in Black*!

And since she wasn't allowed to frighten the locals, she took up the new pastime of people-watching. She found herself in an ideal location, what with the constant flow of people from every corner of the country and the world making their pilgrimage to Music City.

Perhaps the Opryland Hotel became one the Dama's preferred haunts because of the familiar sounds of babbling water coming from the fountains in the atrium. For this port dweller, it always comes back to the water, siempre el agua. Despite finding happiness in her new hometown, she can never forget the guayaquileña blood that once coursed through her veins. The nostalgia is enough to lead her, from time to time, to return to the streets she haunted centuries ago. They look much different now, but they are still bathed in the fragrance and the warmth of the river.

Most nights, though, after having a downright good time people-watching at the hotel, the Dama is known to enjoy a stroll along Riverfront Park and watch the city lights flutter on the surface of the river like iridescent watercolors. Whenever she has a hankering for old-fashioned country music, she floats through the walls of the honky-tonks, where she watches aging couples do the two-step, nostalgic for dances and love affairs from bygone days.

If she's in the mood for something a little more of the moment, she appears in the bars on Nashville's Broadway to watch the young (and not so young) tipsily sing along to the latest country hits, covered by bands that dream night after night of making it big.

Outside Legends Corner, an iconic honky-tonk in downtown Nashville, there's a mural where country music's most illustrious stars sit around a table in a bar from another dimension. If you're ever in that part of town, chances are you'll come across the Dama Tapada basking in their smiling faces, sometimes for hours on end, imagining what it would be like to join the party. Sit next to Garth Brooks and Johnny Cash, chit chat with Dolly Parton and Loretta Lynn. Regale them with her tales of seduction and past lives. Imbue them with a little of her guayaquileña aura.

But what she truly longs for, above all, is to have fingers of flesh once again, if only to dip them gently into the Cumberland River, just like the mangroves whose roots reach down into the waters of the Río Guayas.

Choose your own crónica:

Inventory of an isla en peso

Inventory of the Weight of an Island

Inventory of an isla en peso

La eterna miseria que es el acto de recordar.

"La isla en peso," Virgilio Piñera

One of those Miami nights, one German boyfriend, and one parking garage downtown. From the other side of the car window, the attendant says to him, "Caballero, se le cayó la sonrisa." *Poesía microscópica:* with his Cuban rhythm, *son del areíto*, the aging prophet foretells that our relationship is doomed.

Two plates of tostones at Versailles. Three escritoras, one Cuban, one Puerto Rican, and one Ecuadorian, *en la mesa del café.* Beneath the warmth of the chandeliers, *la noche invade con su olor* and the writer friends laugh, conspire, and share *las eternas historias de estas tierras*: book fairs, writing programs, and the ever-present mansplaining. *La claridad mueve las lenguas.*

Three and a half seasons of the *La Tremenda Corte* in black and white. Suffocating family lunches with Tres Patines and Nananina in the background. One holy, catholic, and apostolic childhood: "¡A la reja!" *El mediodía estático se mueve, se balancea.*

Five orders of ropa vieja at a Cuban restaurant in Guayaquil and one psychologist that escorts his patients to rehab centers in Havana. He's returned to Ecuador bursting at the seams with stories, *todas esas historias*: the only one he manages to recreate for his three daughters is the dish with the funny name, *el nombre más querido*.

Fourteen passengers and one aluminum dinghy. Four survivors with *el mar picando en sus espaldas*. One little boy, two countries, and one INS raid in Little Havana. From a student apartment not far from the very same *sitio dejado por su sombra*, the three sisters stare at the image of the boy hero. Elián's *hora terrible* gone viral. Pobrecito niño. Trapped between *dos maracas pulsadas diestramente*.

Twenty-two Cuban sandwiches at La Carreta. One airport and two student visas. *El primer contacto carnal*: dalliances stolen from the archive of memory. *El horroroso paseo circular* of goodbyes *en este país donde no hay animales salvajes*.

Fifty cats ninety miles north of Cuba. One Spanish boyfriend. One photo at the buoy marking the southernmost point, one Mardi Gras, and one Hemingway house seen only from the outside. *La noche se cruza de paralelos* and *el solitario curso del amor* doesn't survive the drive back to Miami.

Two hundred and seventy minutes of live footage of the rafts broadcast between *Despierta América* and the daytime telenovelas. Wet feet, dry feet. *En el momento en que nadie cree en Dios*, the sisters pray that all of them will get to shore. So close they can feel *el peso de una isla en el amor de un pueblo*. The telenovelas have long gone off the air, so have the sisters. All that remains is *la maldita circunstancia del agua por todas partes*.

Inventory of the Weight of an Island

The never-ending torment that is the act of remembering
"The Weight of the Island," Virgilio Piñera

One of those Miami nights, one German boyfriend, and one parking garage downtown. From the other side of the car window, the attendant says to him, "Caballero, se le cayó la sonrisa." *A microscopic poem:* with his Cuban rhythm, *rhythm of the areíto*, the aging prophet foretells that our relationship is doomed.

Two plates of tostones at Versailles. Three escritoras, one Cuban, one Puerto Rican, and one Ecuadorian, *at the table in the café*. Beneath the warmth of the chandeliers, *the night rushes in with its scent* and the writer friends laugh, conspire, and share *the never-ending stories of this land*: book fairs, writing programs, and the ever-present mansplaining. *The glow of the light moves tongues.*

Three and a half seasons of *La Tremenda Corte* in black and white. Suffocating family lunches with Tres Patines and Nananina in the background. One holy, catholic, and apostolic childhood: ¡A la reja! *The static height of noon bobs and shifts.*

Five orders of ropa vieja at a Cuban restaurant in Guayaquil and one psychologist that escorts his patients to rehab centers in Havana. He's returned to Ecuador bursting at the seams with stories, *all those stories*: the only one he manages to recreate for his three daughters is the dish with the funny name, *the most cherished name*.

Fourteen passengers and one aluminum dinghy. Four survivors with *the sea prodding them in their backs*. One little boy, two countries, and one INS raid in Little Havana. From a student apartment not far from the very same *spot left by his shadow*, the three sisters stare at the image of the boy hero. Elián's *dreadful hour* gone viral. Pobrecito niño. Trapped between *two deftly shaken maracas*.

Twenty-two Cuban sandwiches at La Carreta. One airport and two student visas. *The first fleshly encounter*: dalliances stolen from the archive of memory. *The frightful revolving loop* of goodbyes *in this country where there are no wild animals*.

Fifty cats ninety miles north of Cuba. One Spanish boyfriend, one photo at the buoy marking the southernmost point, one Mardi Gras, and one Hemingway house seen only from the outside. *The night crosses lines of latitude* and *love's lonely course* doesn't survive the drive back to Miami.

Two hundred and seventy minutes of live footage of the rafts broadcast between *Despierta América* and the daytime telenovelas. Wet feet, dry feet. *When no one believes in God*, the sisters pray that all of them will get to shore. So close they can feel *the weight of an island in the love of a people*. The telenovelas have long gone off the air, so have the sisters. All that remains is *the godforsaken fate of being surrounded by water*.

Country Roads

With his front paws pressed up against the glass, Roscoe scans the trees looking for squirrels. He becomes agitated when he spots a raccoon, barking as if to make it clear that he'd rather be out there chasing after anything that moves. Soon he calms down, realizing that it's not so bad to be stuck sitting on his owner's lap. He remembers how much he likes to squish his snout against the A.C. vent and starts to enjoy the ride.

His owner, Adam, makes a half-hearted attempt to push Roscoe onto the backseat, but the truth is he likes having him close. He runs his fingers through the dog's wiry fur as he drives. He adores this mutt, his trusty companion on every road trip and fishing excursion.

It's a Sunday afternoon, and they're on their way to Adam's grandparents' house. Despite having to cross the border between two states, the trip only takes an hour. His entire family lives in a tiny town in southwestern Kentucky, nestled in an idyllic hollow of the Appalachian Mountains. The landscape of smooth peaks, forests, and ponds unfolds along the side of the highway. The mountains steal the show with their spectacular tapestry dappled with cool colors. A faint, smoky blue haze drapes itself over them like gauze, perhaps to heal the wounds that fracking has left behind.

A spring appears, wedged between the highway and the mountains, just before the entrance to a tunnel. It's not uncommon to see people, jugs in hand, getting their fill of freshwater. In the lanes to the left, herds of pick-up trucks whiz by. Like an army of Goliaths, everything about them is oversized. The tires, the bumpers, even the dogs riding inside. Adam uses the term *gigantor* to refer both to the vehicles and their occupants.

The big steel bullies proudly sport bumper stickers supporting their respective football teams. Some are for the University of Tennessee, others for the University of Kentucky. Some have deer symbols and the logos of Bass Pro Shops and Cabela's. Stickers supporting Republican candidates can be spotted along with the occasional confederate flag. But among the stick families and miscellaneous emblems, the most abundant bumper stickers of all are the religious ones containing a psalm, a cross, or the famous Jesus fish.

Adam has invented a game to pass the time: reading the messages on the Baptist church signs before they fly by. There's always a surprise—like Forrest Gump's box of chocolates—but some are more bitter than others. They range from traditional declarations like "Jesus saves" to witty quips like "God sent the first text message: the Bible." The spelling errors are part of the charm.

Adam would have liked to have been named Larry like his father or Paul like his grandfather, but his mother had a different idea. Sometimes he thinks his name came laden with expectations, and he's not sure if he's managed to meet them. In any case, his mother likes to say that life gave her a son who's a bit of an odd man out. She's told him this directly more than once, and she's been known to expound upon how she always knew that God sent her a very special boy.

With the exception of his love of fishing, Adam has always felt out of place. He doesn't share any of the other pastimes or beliefs that seem to be universal where he grew up. He doesn't even like the same foods. When people ask him why he doesn't move to a more liberal area, he replies that it's because of the lakes. He happens to have been born and raised in one of the best regions of the country for sport fishing. And as much as he hates to admit it, he likes living near his family.

His grandparents' house comes into view beyond the hill, next to the train tracks. Roscoe notices a *gigantor* dog scraping at the window of a passing pick-up truck and immediately starts to tremble, growling and baring his teeth. Adam hugs him and pats his back, asking Roscoe to be nice. Then he steps on the gas.

"Don't forget," he says to me. "Roscoe is a very special dog."

November Colors

The sky and the lakes seem menacing with their fierce shades of blue. Maybe they feel like stirring things up a little by contrasting with the red leanings of this Smoky Mountain region. Cropping up amid the potbellied pumpkins and smiling scarecrows is sign after sign emblazoned with the name of the Republican presidential candidate. The trees prefer to keep their opinions to themselves, and their leaves have barely changed color, confused by the unseasonably high temperatures this fall. A rustic autumn backdrop to distract me on the hour-long drive to the university where I teach Spanish.

On campus, red, white, and blue signs encourage the students to exercise their right to vote. Curious squirrels inspect the placards, but quickly turn up their noses when no food is to be found. For them, this is just another fall day. I peer up at the glass-enclosed pedestrian bridge that crosses over one of the town's main roads. Several young people march towards their designated polling place as residents of university housing. They're required to travel in groups; it's a safety measure put into place after polling revealed that the student body favored the Democratic candidate.

I chat with a few of the students after our intermediate Spanish class is over. All of them are Southern twentysomethings and optimistic about their generation. They tell me that, even though they share the same religious and conservative values as the culture in which they grew up, they're open to different perspectives and willing to try to understand the other side. For them, this, in and of itself, is a break with their parents' way of thinking. They also trust the democratic process and the checks and balances between the different branches of government. After all, they tell me, their country has already survived a few presidential disasters. They don't think this time around will be any different.

My next stop is the Language and Culture Resource Center. Relegated to the basement of one of the oldest buildings on campus, the LCRC, as it's more commonly known, provides services to the Hispanic immigrant community that lives in the area. I have coffee with the center's director, an Argentine woman who's lived in this Appalachian corner of Tennessee for over two decades. She tells me that this is the first time she can vote in a US election, and flashes a broad, satisfied smile. Not only does she see it as a civic duty, but now more than ever she thinks we need to support diversity and tolerance in this country with the power of our vote. Palabras simples. Asuntos complicados.

A blanket of smoke eerily floats across the landscape, spoiling the view on my drive home. I can't see the mountains anymore. The incessant sound of fire engine sirens drowns everything else out. They're headed to calm the forest fires burning throughout the area.

A gray mass unfurls its tentacles, and I am struck with a sense of certainty that, no matter what, no one will be happy with the outcome.

Later that night, I follow the election results from my in-laws' home in the middle of Kentucky. They are a liberal-leaning family, not quite what you'd expect in this part of the country. My mother-in-law stares, incredulous, at the television screen; my father-in-law takes refuge in the strings of an electric guitar. My husband's grandfather, a 90-year-old Navy veteran, squints his eyes, scrunches up his nose, and shrugs his shoulders in resignation. He already fulfilled his duty to his country and achieved the American dream. Now it's the next generation's turn to take up the baton.

How to Be an Online Spanish Instructor

Click here. Click there. Open the document. Review it, click again, enter the grade. Repeat these steps twenty-three times. Click to accept work submitted after the due date. Click, click, click, click. Much easier than unleashing a litany of claims of ignorance and over-the-top excuses. Click, click, click, click. Grade like a robot. If you grade like a person, te puedes meter en problemas. Sprinkle in a comment here and there. Be sure to keep your notes brief. It's almost certain that they won't even read them. Be strict enough so you don't raise any red flags about grade inflation but be careful! You don't want to get a reputation for being a difficult instructor. [*There's even a website where they can rate us for* hotness, *for goodness' sake.*] Click, click, click, click. But most of all, remember that the students enrolled in this class are just checking a box, fulfilling a few required credits so they can get their hands on that coveted, overvalued piece of paper.

Ghosts of New Years Past

Adam had the kind of treehouse and bicycle adventures with his friends that Latin American children of the eighties would dream about as we devoured *E.T.* and *The Goonies* alongside mountains of popcorn. And, as if that weren't enough, his childhood was set against a picturesque backdrop of forests and mountains, crystal-blue lakes and skies . . . everything that my urban childhood was not.

It's here in this dreamlike place where Adam grew up, a small town nestled in the southern Appalachian mountains, where I'll ring in the new year. It will arrive surrounded by absolute stillness. No fireworks. No celebratory burning of effigies of the old year like we do in Ecuador. None of the gleeful mayhem of the port city of Guayaquil or the swollen crowds of people on the beaches of Salinas.

With every fin de año that I spend away from my country, I miss the spectacle of the glowing skies and the chaos that my Spanish students react to with a mix of humor and eloquence, saying, "Eso solo pasa aquí cuando hay un riot, Señora Márquez." I can't say they're wrong.

In the video I show the class, booming sounds reverberate from barges out on the water, and we can practically feel the heat from the flares dancing on the sand.

It's as if there on the warm shores caressed by the Pacific, the world were about to end.

I wonder if the same thought crossed Adam's mind as we waited on a seventh-floor beachfront balcony for the new year to begin. Scarcely daring to breathe, he wordlessly observed the pyrotechnic choreography that splayed across the black sky.

Thousands of sparks formed flower petals and fiery cascades.

The tumult above contrasted with the still waters below.

Around midnight, when people started to drag papier-mâché effigies of the old year into the gigantic piles rising at the foot of the sea, he whispered in my ear: "Do they really have to burn them?"

I stroked his back. Cuando era pequeña, tampoco me hacía mucha gracia que quemaran a los viejos.

As Adam grieved the passing of the giant paper dolls, champagne shot from bottles on the balconies around us, and everyone ate the traditional twelve grapes, washing them down with long lists of desires and regrets disguised as resolutions.

The following December, it will be Adam's turn to console me, this time for the deafening lack of alboroto on New Year's Eve.

With a little bit of luck, the echoes of the Appalachians will bring me wind of the Nochevieja festivities on the Ecuadorian coast. The boom from a barge, wishes of *¡Feliz año!* from the lips of family and friends, or, if I'm lucky, the nostalgic song of an effigy of the old year, humming as it calmly waits for the flames to embrace it. Only by burning can it fulfill its fleeting destiny, offering us the chance for a fresh start, reminding us of long-held dreams that may still be within reach.

An old year sacrificed in exchange for twelve months to reinvent ourselves.

Chronicles of My Own Personal Narnia

An average day. The kind where you wake up late, frustrated that you succumbed to the seductive allure of a Netflix binge. The kind where you discover, to your horror, that there's no more coffee right as your phone dings with a reminder about the appointment to replace the spare tire that your car's been limping around on for the past week.

As you rush out the door on this average day, you bang your elbow and then your knee, which is how you discover that you code-switch even when you curse. [*Maldito motherfucker!*] Ten minutes later, on the way to the tire shop, you swear that the weather is trying to mess with you. It knows all too well that your body, acostumbrado al calor guayaquileño, has had it up to here with this Narnia-esque cold.

You think about Lucy, the curious little girl who enters a wardrobe and comes out the other side in a different world. A strange, faraway place, stuck in a terrible winter under the spell of the White Witch.

The Michelin Man welcomes you and reminds you that it's time to shed those extra pounds you put on during the holidays.

Fabuloso.

Even though you're there early, you still have to wait. No hay problema. You've come armed with a good book, one of your Christmas gifts to yourself. Its pages contain the lectures on literature that Julio Cortázar gave at Berkeley in the eighties, which just so happens to be your favorite decade.

You settle into the waiting room, whose chairs are arranged in a circle of worship around the TV God. The background noise grates on your nerves, but you try your best to immerse yourself in the Argentine author's master class on fantasy stories.

You imagine shattering the limits of time and space, and suddenly there you are in the front row of the lecture hall, la más fan entre todas las fans de Julito. You raise your hand to ask Cortázar about the nationality of the Cronopios.

He turns to look at you.

And right in that instant, as if in a poorly-written story, something snaps you out of your reverie.

First, a series of sharp sounds cause a stabbing pain in your head—surely due to your lack of sleep—and right away you realize it's the voice of a Fox News reporter. As if she were bothered by what you were reading and decided to intrude your thoughts.

So, you start listening.

She hits all the buzz words:

Immigration

Undocumented

DACA

Latinos

Like a flash of lightning, the words cut through your caffeine-deficient fog, and you abruptly return to the real world.

You look around you, and it's as if you just now noticed that the other chairs are occupied by creatures even whiter than the Michelin Man. [*Instead of the Michelin Man, I'm imagining the villainous Stay-Puft Marshmallow Man from* Ghostbusters.]

And you're seated right in the center of the circle with your not-so-white skin.

Con tu libro en español.

You forgot that the inhabitants of this southern Narnia are ice statues under the spell of the White Witch, who doesn't like tropical creatures bringing color to her winter.

You also forgot that here in your own personal Narnia—complete with a landscape straight out of a fantasy story—they don't like you speaking Spanish.

Interpreting the American Dream

Day 1

A vibrant rainbow spills over the string of small mountains, high-lighting the blue and gold brushstrokes that span the sky. In this corner of Tennessee, the beauty of the Appalachians is sometimes overwhelming. Buen trabajo, Dios, ¡mensaje recibido! I can almost understand the religious fervor of the locals. Almost.

I check the time on my phone and impatiently drum my fingers on the steering wheel. My calculation of twelve minutes proved to be wrong. Maldito Walmart. One of your enormous tractor trailers is disrupting the typically unhurried pace of traffic along Main Street, which leads to a quaint little downtown that looks like a time cap-sule. It has a string of petite brick buildings, antique shops, and other small businesses. A boutique's window display contains a surrealistic scene of headless mannequins in outfits that seem to have escaped from the eighties. [*Your favorite decade.*]

My destination comes into view after going over the railroad tracks. I make a right and find myself in front of what looks like a warehouse. Its institutional look stands out here in the middle of the Bible Belt. The woman from the interpreter agency has called me three times already to remind me that I should arrive fifteen minutes before the appointment time. Her español de España is still buzz-ing in my ear. I give myself a once-over in the rearview mirror and hustle to get out of the car, accidentally leaving my book and water bottle behind.

A young, red-haired woman greets me from behind the reception desk. The bouncy curls that frame her face seem to have a much happier disposition than she does. I declare that I'm the interpreter for a patient named Iván Jiménez. She shoots me a look, and I can't tell if she's confused or constipated. I provide more details from the agency—I almost start pronouncing my Zs and Js with the Iberian accent of the scheduler—but the young woman's face is glued to her phone. She just nods and points to the waiting area.

I leaf through some of the magazines piled on top of the side table. They're the usual waiting room suspects in this part of the country: *Megachurchgoing Family*, *Men Who Hunt*, and the classic *Fishing for Jesus*. Bueno, no exactamente, pero por ahí van. I wish I had the book I left in the car, but my only other option is to scroll on my phone. Twenty minutes later, the patient appears.

How do I know it's him?

The two of us are the only people in the room with a skin tone that you wouldn't expect to see among the cast of the next vampire movie. [*Cindy, is that you?*]

We're ushered into an open area that looks like a gym for senior citizens, not only because of the antiquated exercise equipment, but also because of the people using it. Several speakers are mounted on the walls like elk heads. They vibrate with a genre of music that, to the uninitiated, might sound like soft rock. Simple, pleasant songs that could make for nice background music, except the lyrics aren't exactly light. On the contrary, they have to do with a Father, a Son, sacrifice, and blood.

I bob my head to the rhythm and feel a sudden urge to dance.

Day 3

"¿Por qué este señor odia tanto a los hispanos?" From his seat in the waiting room, Iván Jiménez points at the glowing screen of his iPhone.

A professional interpreter must stay within the bounds of their designated role.
I smile politely and immediately return to the comfort of my book. Little do I know that this false sense of safety is about to be crushed to bits, just like the crackers that the ladies behind the reception desk are chomping on.

Day 5

After completing his physical therapy exercises, a heating pad brings Iván Jiménez some relief. But it's not enough. Frustration creeps across his face like a viny weed growing out of his pain. I recite whole passages from the interpreter handbook in my head, like a mantra. My eyes are glued to my book.

"¿Está leyendo en inglés?" the patient asks me. There's a hint of urgency in his voice, as if the vine were tightening around his throat.

A professional interpreter does not share personal information with the patient.
I nod my head, just barely. I look around as if to make sure the Spanish woman from the agency can't see me. I return to my book: my liferaft.

"Usted estudió aquí, ¿cierto?"

Iván Jiménez's eyes expect a response. Why is good fortune bestowed at random? What do we make of the different portions of the American dream we've been allotted?

The ruthless vine grows and squeezes. I excuse myself and practically leap toward the water cooler, where I decide to stay put as I wait for the physical therapist to return. I can't escape the thorny grip of the weed. Me araña, leaving behind a sense of guilt that I won't be able to shake off for a long time.

I breathe in, breathe out.

I try to focus on the song that's playing on the speakers in every corner. A new mantra. *Oh, how He loves us. Oh, how He loves us. Oh, how He loves.*

Day 7

I don't bring a book to the appointments anymore.

As I wait to be called back, I stare at my phone screen and try to find it as enticing as it seems to be to the young receptionist, her green eyes captivated by a stream of likes and selfies.

"El tratamiento no está dando resultados, el dolor no ha disminuido." I do my best to interpret the patient's complaint with a neutral expression on my face. But I can already foresee what's coming.

It takes the physical therapist a few seconds to remember that they shouldn't look at me when they're speaking, and finally they look at the patient—a forced smile failing to conceal their irritation—and proceed to read the notes from Iván Jiménez's chart as evidence that, up until now, the patient has reported consistent improvement.

I'm not a mediator, that's not my role. But I sense that both of them are expecting me to do just that right now.

Iván Jiménez ends up apologizing. He admits that he's frustrated; he just wants the pain to go away, to leave him in peace. So I say that the patient wants to continue with the treatment plan. The physical therapist's attempt at a smile is more fruitful this time, and they step away to schedule the rest of the sessions.

I let my guard down ever so briefly, but it's long enough for Iván Jiménez to lean toward me, lower his voice, and say that immigration has detained one of his friends, and they're going to deport him in a few days.

Me dice que tiene miedo.

A professional interpreter should notify all parties present that everything they say will be interpreted.

I look at Iván Jiménez. I try to say with my eyes, which are the same color as his, everything I can't say out loud.

The physical therapist comes back. I jot down the dates and times of the next appointments in my notebook, and I forget to interpret the last thing the patient said. Today is one of those days when I just don't have it in me to be professional.

The Two Sides of the Park

Roscoe happily trots through the grass, dry leaves crunching underfoot. Fred Miller Park is one of his favorite spots in Morristown, Tennessee, and he only pauses his lighthearted romp when he stumbles upon a pair of long wooden tables.

To the left, two grease-stained boxes emblazoned with a red, white, and blue logo sit prominently at the center of a small feast, complete with hefty bottles of a dark, sugary liquid.

To the right, golden tortillas are piled high and dense salsas sparkle in the sunlight, while a tantalizing aroma drifts over from the grill and big trumpet riffs reverberate from a tiny source.

The two families, each one tucked into their respective corner of a single patch of grass, enjoy the indiscriminately pleasant surroundings: willows and birches swaying in the breeze like a prayer, swings creaking in harmony with the squeals of the children.

The two families are so close, they could reach out their arms and touch one another. Speak to one another.

But behind this scene there are years of avoiding eye contact.

Countless years of pretending the ones on the other side don't exist.

Roscoe, a rescue mutt and a stranger to human boundaries, ventures into the space between the tables, sniffing expectantly. A nibble of crust or a sliver of meat—he'd be happy with either.

Heads turn, observing his frantic search as he silently transgresses the line between the neighbors.

The same line that divides the park in half and breaks the heart of the city in two.

One Hundred Cornfields of Solitude

When you're from one of the most dangerous cities in Latin America, your safety mode gets activated every time you go back to visit. As if you could keep danger away simply by staying alert: a sort of self-defense state of zen.

Back in your little mountain town in Tennessee—even though a tiny voice inside you reminds you that danger is always lurking for a woman, no matter where she is—you allow yourself to let down your guard a little.

You relax.

You feel safe again.

Then the universe offers you a new zip code. The opportunity of a lifetime: an MFA in creative writing at a famous university in a small town in the Midwest, among the cornfields.

You let your guard down even more. The City of Literature. A mecca for anyone with literary ambitions in this country. A paradise filled with writers.

Nothing bad could happen in a place like that.

Right?

But shortly after arriving, you encounter a world ruled by slumlords that no one warned you about. A place where the façades parade as houses—complete with porches and flowerbeds—but behind their doors they conceal small, sad apartments owned by corporations headquartered in some metropolis far beyond the cornfields.

You discover that your life and your safety are of no concern to these corporate entities, who subcontract maintenance services to other companies who then, in turn, subcontract the work to men who answer to no one. This absolves all parties of responsibility. No one is accountable. Are you given any assurances about the men that have access to where you live? Absolutely not.

A few weeks after classes begin, you ask the corporate entity to replace the broken toilet in the studio apartment that they've leased to you. They send a stalker to your door: a man who accuses you of stealing the money that, according to him, he accidentally dropped in your postage stamp-sized bathroom.

A stalker who pounds on your door several times throughout the day.

A stalker that you find later that evening . . . circling the parking lot . . . waiting for you.

A stalker that makes you feel trapped in your own car and prompts you to call the police for the first time in your life.

A stalker who completely obliterates your safety mode.

But the story doesn't end here.

You discover that your life is of no concern to the police, either. The officer that they send twenty minutes after you call 9-1-1 files your case under the one that he finds more pressing: the stalker's lost property report. You wait in vain for some sign that the danger has passed, but all the officer gives you is his business card. In case you find the stalker's money.

And, no, it doesn't end here with this other man, the officer.

Having taken shelter at a hotel a few hours after the incident with the stalker and the police officer, the first person that you contact is the director of your program. The hours crawl by at a snail's pace as you wait for her to respond to your email recounting everything you've just experienced. You tell her you don't know what to do. That you're afraid. You just arrived, and you don't know anyone else here.

You imagine comforting words, compassion, support. Maybe even empathy. You cling to this hope, a glimmer of light in the middle of one of your darkest days.

But instead of light, the program director offers you links. She is out of the country and won't return until the end of the semester. She copies the department chair and washes her hands of the situation. She also suggests that you reach out to other women in your program. She never contacts you again after that.

The department chair immediately sends you more links and phone numbers. You won't hear from her again until several weeks later, after you've moved to a new apartment on the other side of town. Her unhurried and half-hearted attempt at appearing supportive is like salt in the wound.

You meet with one of the women in your program at a pub. Before you can finish telling her what happened to you, she interrupts you to tell you that something else must be going on here. That some repressed memory from your past is making you feel this way.

No one raped you.

No one touched you.

What happened to you wasn't all that serious.

Then she takes a last sip of her IPA, gets up from the barstool, and leaves.

The only thing that anyone you contact at the university does is flood your inbox with more links and phone numbers. Every time you ask someone for help, links. At the end of every appointment, more links and more phone numbers. No one offers you a way out of this giant corn maze of numbers and links, and for a time you feel trapped in a cruel game designed solely to follow protocols and avoid liabilities for the university.

As if those links could replace comforting words and actual support. As if those numbers could protect you and offer you the one thing you desperately need: a place to feel safe.

After surviving a series of dismissive responses and finding your own way out of that godforsaken corn maze, you make a promise to yourself.

You will never be dismissive when a woman tells you that she is afraid.

You'll demand action by her side and on her behalf, over and over again, until it's impossible for them to go on ignoring your voices. Until the day comes when every woman reaches her hand out to another woman in danger. Until all women learn to take care of one another. Until no woman feels alone—whether she finds herself surrounded by cornfields or in a tranquil city, or in one of the most dangerous cities in the world.

No woman alone, ever again.

Belonging

When you're given your appointment to take the United States citizenship exam, you start studying and preparing for it. You read and memorize lists. Names. Dates.

Just like you used to do before tests in school and exams in college, except this time you find audio flashcards on YouTube and listen to them over and over during the ten-hour trip from Iowa City to Nashville.

What is the economic system in the United States? The passing silos and barns help you stay focused, until you come across a small army of cardboard cutout babies emerging from the cornfields. There is something sinister in their smiles. You can almost hear them singing "Choose Life" to the tune of "One, two, Freddy's coming for you," but you don't complain because that's part of the pact you make when you live here. And besides, it helps you remember question ten:

What is freedom of religion?

You pass the Gateway Arch in Saint Louis having memorized the thirteen original states. You gradually leave behind that peculiar, flat landscape that is the Midwest. Where the sky is aggressively vast. A sky that bites and that, at times, you've even thought might swallow you whole.

When the GPS welcomes you to Tennessee, your heart practically does a somersault. Meanwhile, you can now recite all the states that border Canada. By the time the AT&T Building peeks out from the Nashville skyline, you've finally got a handle on the one question that you've been stumbling over: *The House of Representatives has how many voting members?*

You make a mental note to look up the names of the senators that represent your state, something that the YouTube flash cards can't tell you. They also can't tell you the answer to *Who is the governor of your state now?* But you don't need to look that one up. It's a surname you know well, one you used to see embossed on plaques all over the University of Tennessee campus.

The next video reminds you that they will also ask you questions unrelated to civics or geography or history. Questions about your personal life. You're compelled to prepare for those, too, because you aren't quite sure how to answer some of them.

For example: *Where do you currently live?*

You're careful to rehearse this one because you don't want to set off any alarms in a federal building in Nashville.

Your husband lives in Tennessee and you . . . live in Iowa?

You're worried that the immigration officers will be suspicious of any pauses or hesitations when the time comes to respond to this question, because the truth is, even though your current zip code places you squarely in the Corn State, you don't think of yourself as someone who lives in Iowa.

"How is it that you live in Tennessee, but you're here in Iowa?" Valeria Luiselli asks you at an event held by your writing program.

You smile knowingly.

She isn't the first person to be confused by your answer. It reminds you of how your Elementary Spanish I students would answer what seemed like a straightforward question: "¿Dónde vives?" They would fill in the blank on the test with the name of a place that didn't correspond to the physical location of the university. The name of a place that they considered Home.

You would roll your eyes.

They didn't understand the question, you used to think. Don't they realize that they live in the dorms next door? How else could they roll out of bed and come to class in their pajama pants?

But it turns out, you're the one who didn't understand.

Years later, it finally makes sense, because now you're living the same conundrum yourself: I *go to school* in Iowa. I *live* in Tennessee.

This is the answer you give to the officer assigned to conduct your naturalization interview and exam in Nashville. She barely looks at you, her face fixed on the screen in front of her, her fingers typing into an official record. In five minutes, she knows everything about you, but all you know about her is where she went to college, because it's displayed on the beige diploma that's almost indistinguishable against the drab, vanilla walls of the office.

Suddenly, the typing stops.

You're sure it's a delayed reaction to the last thing you said. You feel the muscles in your back become tense.

"I can't find the address for the University of Iowa," she says. You give her the information she needs and resume breathing, hoping that the worst is behind you.

You successfully answered the exam questions.

Your personal information and fingerprints didn't raise any red flags.

You can see the light at the end of the tunnel. You start to relax.

Down the hall, your husband is sitting in a chair, waiting for you. Down the street, two seats at a bar wait for you both. It's one of the many surrounding Nashville tourist traps with live country-pop music, a musical genre he doesn't particularly like but will tolerate for your sake. Especially on a day like today when you should be celebrating.

Soon, all you'll have to remember are song lyrics.

You can almost taste the beer and hear the music.

But what follows is a game show from hell that you'll be forced to play over the stretch of the longest five minutes of your life:

Have you ever been a member of the Communist Party, the Nazi Party, or a terrorist organization?

Were you ever involved in any way with genocide?

Were you ever involved in any way with torture?

Have you ever been a prostitute or procured anyone for prostitution?

Do you support the US Constitution and the US government?

Will you obey the laws of the United States?

Are you willing to take the Oath of Allegiance to the United States?

Are you willing to bear arms on behalf of the United States?

Would you be willing to defend the United States in a war?

Were you . . .?

Are you . . .?

Will you . . .?

You want to request a time-out. A glass of water. A short break, please, just for a minute. But the officer keeps going and you don't want to cause any trouble so you blurt out "No" and "I am" and "I will" over and over until she's satisfied, and you pray that it will all be over soon and that you'll never have to go through something like this ever again.

When the officer congratulates you on passing the citizenship exam, you don't feel as happy as you'd thought you would.

Of course, you feel relieved and excited. Tennessee is your Home, and you're overjoyed to make the relationship official. Nevertheless, you're left with a taste of guilt in your mouth, a trace of sadness, as if you've just betrayed someone very important to you.

Someone who you don't see much anymore, whose presence you miss less and less, but who still loves you just the same. As you walk back down the hallway that you nervously walked up a half hour earlier, you ask that someone for forgiveness.

You promise that you won't forget them. You thank them for the Sundays at abuela's house, the slumber parties with girlfriends from school, the first loves. The tropical posadas at Christmastime and the New Year's celebrations at the beach.

You insist that you'll visit them soon, that you'll dedicate a poem to them. Maybe even two.

Even though they'll no longer appear in your official record in this country, they'll always be part of your story. A story for which you'll never have to study or rehearse.

Later, at the bar on Nashville's Broadway, the beer and the music both go down with a slightly bitter taste.

Visitor's Guide

Guayaquil:

Constant, round-the-clock noise. A school where the main subjects are bullying and a religion rife with contradictions. Patacones, tortillas de verde. Buildings looming over a street leading to a bank job downtown. Factories lining a road leading to an office job in the nearby city of Daule. Hordes of guayaquileños in Salinas for New Year's Eve, overlooking the Pacific Ocean and what appears to be the end of the world. Humidity. Sweat. Sofoque.

Miami:

Pure heat, decadence, demasiado, a comfortable but misleading introduction to the United States. Ocean Drive, Art Deco, a fiery sunrise over the Atlantic. A purgatory from which you surely won't want to be delivered.

Tennessee:

One long chain of mountains as blue as the clouds that surround them. The hills, a never-ending patchwork quilt. [*As you wrote before, once again "the pattern silently but relentlessly repeats itself, over and over."*] Whiskey and moonshine. Dolly Parton with her guitar. Extrañeza. Otherness. Signs demanding four more years for *their* president alongside Confederate flags. Dolly again. Dolly forever. Roads dotted with tiny churches, none of them Catholic. Both a sanctuary and a shock to your sense of identity. The chill of sweet tea hitting your teeth. Where the Río Guayas meets the Cumberland River, and the Dama Tapada haunts the streets of Nashville disguised as the Lady in Black. Where you will discover your voice.

Iowa City:

A sky so vast it'll swallow you whole [*As you wrote before, it's "a sky that bites."*]. You'll be all alone among the cornfields, the surprisingly good beer and bar food your only solace. Elitism and exclusion. A place where some women turn a blind eye to other women's pain. Silos going by in the car window. Writing workshops that bring the highest of highs and the lowest of lows. Bone-piercing cold and dirty snow. A harrowing siren warning of an approaching tornado. A white rabbit winking at you before disappearing into the snow.

San Diego:

Ocean, mountains, perfect weather. Scenery straight out of a Hollywood movie—cheery, swaying palm trees included. This is the somewhat unsettling landscape of toomuchness that will welcome you to a new job in a new zip code on the other side of the country. "So, you're a California girl now?" a fellow writer will ask you when you run into each other at a book fair in New York City. "But isn't your whole thing that you're a South American who writes from *the South*?" Who are you going to be now? is the implied question that you'll ask yourself, attempting to solve this latest riddle with equal parts eagerness and fear, as you start your new job at a university library that resembles a spaceship. Una nave-biblioteca with the nonsensical legacy of Dr. Seuss tucked away in its special collections deck. Faithful to its brutalist architecture, it will be a shock to your senses, much in the same way this city will be a shock to your introverted ways. This time, you'll find yourself sitting next to a different bronze statue: the Cat in the Hat and its creator. You'll gaze upon the strange building with a thousand looking-glass windows, like the one Alice encountered in her second act. Here you'll shed your leaves once again, reinvent yourself anew, as you explore your ever-shifting identity. Don't panic if you feel disoriented, un tanto fuera de lugar. The blue lakes and soft peaks of your mountain home will always be your compass, leading you back to Wonderland.

Words of Gratitude

Many heartfelt thanks to: Maria Maloney of Mouthfeel Press, for her belief in this project and for being an example of how publishers can support writers as well as translators; Sacha Idell of *The Southern Review*, who is perhaps the nation's most attentive, insightful, and considerate translation editor of a literary magazine; Maria Mateo of the Observatory of the Spanish language and Hispanic Cultures in the United States at the Instituto Cervantes at Harvard University, which publishes the *Rincón de Traductores / Translator's Corner*; Elle Charisse, host of the podcast *Speaking Tongues* and the thoughtful first reader of this manuscript; Pablo Medina, translator of Virgilio Piñera's poetry—I used his translations of the title of "La isla en peso" as well as the poem's final line; Anne Fisher and my fellow participants in her August 2023 ALTA multilingual translation workshop, whose enthusiasm for "Inventory of an isla en peso" and "Inventory of the Weight of an Island" gave me the idea to include both versions in this collection; Kelsi Vanada and everyone that makes the American Literary Translators Association go 'round; Kyle Maxey and Umair Kazi at The Authors Guild; Bill Johnston and Christina MacSweeney, for being so generous with their time and wisdom; Don Henderson, Michelle Mirabella, Erin Goodman, Edie Adams, and Dorothy Potter Snyder for their companionship, empathy, guidance, and encouragement; Sean Gasper Bye, Helen Walsh, Stephanie Schechner, and my fellow Philadelphia-based translators and Transversalists; Daniela Becerra, for bringing together the three mosqueteras; Melanie Márquez Adams, for a literary friendship and ongoing collaboration that I treasure dearly; Peter, Simon, and Mia, mis tres amores; and my cheer squad of family and friends. I'd also like to honor my high school Spanish teacher, Harriet Halcomb, who sadly is no longer with us. A quarter century ago, she made an exception for me, agreeing to be my adviser for a senior research project on the role of the media in the Elián González case and allowing me to write it in Spanish. She also noticed something exceptional about my interest in Spanish and encouraged me to continue studying the language beyond high school. I never got the chance to tell her that I followed her sage advice.

- E.H.

About the Author

Melanie Márquez Adams is an Ecuadorian American writer. She holds an MFA in Spanish Creative Writing from the University of Iowa where she was an Iowa Arts Fellow. She is the author of the short story collection *Mariposas Negras* and two essay collections, *Querencia* and *El país de las maravillas*. She is also the editor of the anthology *Del Sur al Norte: Narrativa y Poesía de Autores Andinos*, winner of a 2018 International Latino Book Award. Her fiction and nonfiction can be found in journals such as *The Southern Review, Puerto del Sol, Laurel Review, Spanglish Voces,* and *Huellas Magazine*. Melanie's latest book is *Anfibias,* a collection of domestic horror stories published by Mouthfeel Press.

About the Translator

Emily Hunsberger translates literature written in Spanish by women authors from all across the Americas, including the United States. Her translations have appeared in *Latin American Literature Today*, *The Southern Review*, *PRISM international*, *The Common*, and *Southwest Review*. From 2017 to 2022, Emily produced *Tertulia*, an independent podcast about Spanish-speaking culture in the United States. She has also published original poetry, reporting, criticism, and research in English and Spanish, with work appearing in *Anfibias Literarias*, *Spanglish Voces*, *Bello Collective*, *Latino Book Review*, and *Estudios del Observatorio / Observatorio Studies*. Emily comes to literary translation with a background in community-based work, international sustainable development, education, and immigrant rights, and she holds a B.A. in Spanish from Cornell University and an M.A. in Spanish from George Mason University. She lives with her family in Philadelphia.

Acknowledgments

Versions of these translated crónicas have previously appeared in various literary journals:

"The Ghost of the South," Laurel Review, 2023.

"One Hundred Cornfields of Solitude," *Rincón de Traductores/ Translators' Corner*, a publication of the Observatory of the Spanish Language and Hispanic Cultures in the United States, part of the Instituto Cervantes at Harvard University, 2022.

"Belonging," *The Southern Review*, 2022.

Many of the translations in Wonderland are based on original texts that previously appeared in the following books:

Enviado especial: veinte escritores hispanos miran hacia Cuba, edited by Hernán Vera Álvarez, Suburbano Ediciones, 2022.

El país de las maravillas: crónicas de mi sueño americano by Melanie Márquez Adams, Instituto Digital César Chávez para el Español en Norteamérica, 2021.

Querencia: crónicas de una latinoamericana en USA by Melanie Márquez Adams, Katakana Editores, 2020.

www.ingramcontent.com/pod-product-compliance
Lightning Source LLC
Chambersburg PA
CBHW030459130626
46549CB00007B/2779